ANIMAL ALLIES

GROUPERS AND MORAY EELS TEAM UP!

BY GLORIA KOSTER

CAPSTONE PRESS
a capstone imprint

Published by Capstone Press, an imprint of Capstone.
1710 Roe Crest Drive, North Mankato, Minnesota 56003
capstonepub.com

Library of Congress Cataloging-in-Publication Data
Names: Koster, Gloria, author.
Title: Groupers and moray eels team up! / by Gloria Koster.
Description: North Mankato, Minnesota : Capstone Press, an imprint of Capstone, [2023] | Series: Animal allies | Includes bibliographical references and index. | Audience: Ages 8 to 11 | Audience: Grades 4-6 | Summary: "One super-fast grouper + one slender eel = a dynamic duo! Discover how two vastly different animal species team up for a successful hunt. With lightning-quick speed and razor-sharp teeth, groupers are skillful hunters of the sea - except when their prey hides in the tiny cracks of coral. Cue the moray eels! These slender and squiggly fish flush out prey from the hidey-holes. And when they do, this dream team feasts! With eye-popping photographs, quick facts, and beyond-the-book back matter, Groupers and Moray Eels Team Up! will have young research writers and wildlife fans rooting for these Animal Allies"-- Provided by publisher.
Identifiers: LCCN 2022052695 (print) | LCCN 2022052696 (ebook) |
ISBN 9781669048886 (hardcover) | ISBN 9781669048831 (paperback) | ISBN 9781669048848 (ebook PDF) | ISBN 9781669048862 (kindle edition) | ISBN 9781669048879 (epub)
Subjects: LCSH: Groupers--Behavior--Juvenile literature. | Morays--Behavior--Juvenile literature. | Mutualism (Biology)--Juvenile literature.
Classification: LCC QL638.S48 K67 2023 (print) | LCC QL638.S48 (ebook) | DDC 597/.43--dc23/eng/20230117
LC record available at https://lccn.loc.gov/2022052695
LC ebook record available at https://lccn.loc.gov/2022052696

Editorial Credits
Editor: Donald Lemke; Designer: Sarah Bennett;
Media Researchers: Rebekah Hubstenberger and Svetlana Zhurkin;
Production Specialist: Katy LaVigne

Image Credits
Alamy: Helmut Corneli, 23, WaterFrame, 14; Dreamstime: Steven Melanson, 7; Getty Images: Antonio Busiello, 16, 24, atese, 11, Csaba Tökölyi, 6, Design Pics/Thomas Kline, 18, Eloi_Omella, 28, ES3N, 21, gorsh13, 17; Shutterstock: Adam Leaders, 5, Drew McArthur, 22, Ellen Hui, 19, frantisekhojdysz, cover (bottom), Image Source Trading Ltd, 9, Joseph M. Bowen, 8, Kim_Briers, cover (top right), Kristina Vackova, 13, Miroslav Halama, 29, Natursports, 12, Rich Carey, 26, Richard Whitcombe, 4, 27, RLS Photo, cover (top left), Tom Goaz, 10, WindVector, 25, Yuliya Chsherbakova (background), cover, back cover, and throughout; Superstock: Pacific Stock–Design Pics/Thomas Kline, 15

All internet sites appearing in back matter were available and accurate when this book was sent to press.

Table of Contents

Words in **bold** are in the glossary.

CHAPTER ONE

The Reef

It is daytime in the warm waters of the coral reef. Many fish swim about. The grouper is active during daylight. Others, like the moray eel, are **nocturnal**. They sleep inside cracks in the walls of the reef.

But what is a reef exactly?

coral grouper

Fish swim in and around a coral reef.

A healthy coral reef in the Red Sea, Egypt

This reef is made of coral. It looks like a plant or a rock. But coral is really made up of tiny animals. These animals are called **polyps**. When polyps die, they get hard. New polyps grow on top. This forms the reef. It provides food and shelter to thousands of creatures. Some are predators. Some are prey.

Groupers and moray eels are predators. They are fierce hunters on their own. But sometimes they hunt together. Each fish has a unique skill. Working together can be even better than hunting alone. That is why the moray eel will wake up this afternoon when the grouper comes calling.

A moray eel emerges from a coral reef.

DID YOU KNOW?

Coral reefs make up just a tiny portion of the ocean floor. But they are home to 25 percent of marine life.

A Scary Pair

Groupers and moray eels are very **aggressive** fish. They are scary-looking creatures.

The grouper family is large. There are about 400 different species. Young groupers often have black and yellow markings. They get darker in color as they get older. Some groupers can **camouflage**. Their many bright colors and patterns match the coral reef. This protects them.

graysby grouper

Groupers have fins. Their eyes are high on their heads. They have bulky bodies, but they vary in size. Their size depends on how old they are. It also depends on their species. The coney grouper is about 1 foot (0.3 meters) long. It weighs about one pound (0.45 kilograms). The largest and most frightening grouper is the goliath. It can grow to be 8 feet (2.4 m) long. It can weigh over 800 pounds (363 kg).

A scuba diver observes a goliath grouper.

Groupers have large mouths. They can suck in prey from far away. Their teeth are as sharp as needles. But they mostly crush their food. They use the bony plates behind their mouths. Groupers like to swallow their prey whole. They are **carnivores**. Their diet includes smaller fish—even other groupers! They also eat **crustaceans** like shrimp and lobster.

coral grouper

The moray eel family is large. There are about 200 different species. The smallest ones are a few inches long. The largest can be 10 feet (3 m) long. They can weigh 65 pounds (29 kg). Moray eels have slender bodies. They look like snakes. They slither like snakes too. It's hard to believe they are really fish.

Moray eels have fins but no scales. Their bodies are covered with a **mucus** layer. This protects them in rocky places. It prevents scratches. Sometimes the mucus is poisonous. Moray eels have many different colors and patterns. Some change color too. This helps them to camouflage. They swim forward and backward, blending in with the reef.

fangtooth moray eel

Moray eels keep their mouths open to breathe. This adds to their frightening look. They have tiny eyes and poor vision. But they have an excellent sense of smell. This helps them hunt in dark water.

Moray eels have two sets of teeth. The razor-sharp teeth in front are pointed backward. Prey cannot slip away. But there are also teeth in their throats. These pull food into their stomachs. A moray eel usually eats its prey in one bite. Sometimes it twists its body around larger prey. Then it tears the flesh apart.

DID YOU KNOW?

Moray eels hide in coral reef caves and crevices. Their homes are called eel pits.

Moray eels feed on other fish and crustaceans. They will even attack smaller moray eels. Like groupers, they are carnivores. In fact, these two fish have the same diet. So why aren't they enemies?

It is probably because they hunt at different times. The grouper hunts in the daytime. The moray eel hunts at night. They also capture prey in different ways. The grouper swims in open water. The moray eel grabs its prey in tight spaces. Both fish are high up on the **food chain**. Hunting alone, each one is successful. Still, there are times when these two creatures **collaborate**.

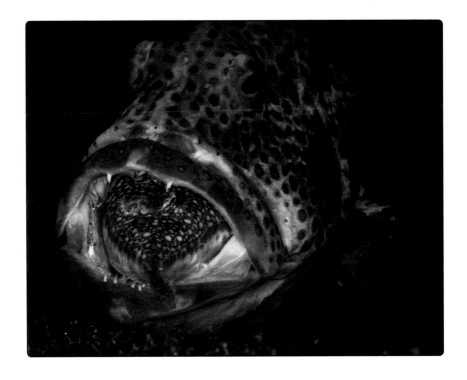

The Hunt

Groupers and moray eels hunt together. Each one plays a part. The grouper takes the lead. It knows where the moray eel lives. Outside the eel's hiding spot, it shakes its head. The shaking is fast. The grouper's dorsal fin stands up. Scientists have observed another behavior too. Sometimes the grouper does a headstand. It uses its body as an arrow. It points in the direction of the prey.

A whitemouth moray eel swims behind a peacock grouper.

The moray eel does not ignore the grouper's
signals. Normally, the moray eel is nocturnal. But
it won't turn down the grouper's invitation. The eel
comes out of its hole. Now the grouper and the moray
eel set out together. The hunt is on!

A Nassau grouper (left) with a green moray eel

Groupers are fast. If their prey stays in open water, they do not need help. But some prey are already hiding. Others escape the grouper during the chase. They take shelter in cracks and crevices. This is when the grouper needs help.

Moray eels are not as fast as groupers. They have a different skill. They can squeeze into tight spaces. They can reach any creature hiding from a grouper. That creature isn't safe anymore.

Who will get the prey? Will it be the grouper? Will it be the moray eel? When these partners team up, two things can happen.

When the moray eel enters a hiding place, the fish inside may escape to open water. It will be mealtime for the waiting grouper. But if the fish doesn't get away, it will be mealtime for the moray eel.

Sometimes the grouper gets the prey. Sometimes it's the moray eel. The winner takes all! There is no sharing. Groupers and moray eels both can swallow their prey whole. There is no food left to fight over. In other situations, they may attack each other. But during the hunt, they play by the same rule.

A peacock grouper captures prey in its mouth.

A moray eel catches a fish.

Could the grouper and moray eel both be winners? This could happen if several fish are hiding. One might come out of the hole. It will end up in the grouper's mouth. Another might remain in the hole. It won't escape the eel's jaws.

DID YOU KNOW?

The partnership between groupers and moray eels was first discovered by Redouan Bshary, a Swiss researcher. He was observing coral reefs in the Red Sea.

CHAPTER FOUR

A Working Relationship

Groupers and moray eels are not true friends. They are more like coworkers.

When they hunt, they act like a tag team. Working together, they catch more prey. How much more? Scientists think they catch five times more.

In school, you may collaborate with classmates. Some group projects require a product. Have you noticed that different students have different abilities? Connecting these abilities can make your product better. This is true for animal partners too. Groupers and moray eels benefit from each other's strengths.

Groupers and moray eels shine in different ways. Groupers have speed. They have excellent eyesight. Moray eels are slower. Their vision is poor. But they have an excellent sense of smell. They have another amazing ability. They can squeeze into holes.

The grouper travels about the reef. It can locate a delicious meal. What if the prey is tucked away? The grouper stays hungry. Should it invite a moray eel to come along? This may not help the grouper every time. But if the fish work together, someone is sure to benefit.

In nature, members of two different species may connect. Their connection is called **symbiosis**. Symbiosis may help one animal but harm the other. It may be good for one without harming the other. Sometimes symbiosis is good for each of them. This type of symbiosis is called **mutualism**. The partnership between groupers and moray eels is an example of mutualism. The relationship helps them both.

CHAPTER FIVE

Predator or Prey?

There are only a few animals that threaten groupers and moray eels. These include barracudas, sharks, and sea snakes. Groupers try to defend themselves from predators. They make rumbling sounds. They use fierce body language. Moray eels may tie their bodies in a knot.

A shark swims above a grouper.

People catch moray eels for food.

Groupers and eels can get sick from **parasites**.
They can be killed by people fishing. Anyone who
eats these fish should be careful. Groupers contain
a high level of **mercury**. Moray eel blood can be
poisonous. It is important to cook it completely.

The coral reef is home to groupers and moray eels. The reef needs protection. Oil spills are harmful to marine life. They can kill shallow water fish. This means less food for groupers and moray eels.

Plastic in the ocean is another huge problem. Sea creatures can swallow plastic particles.

Cutting down trees also affects the reef. It loosens soil near the seashore. The soil slides into the ocean. It smothers the coral.

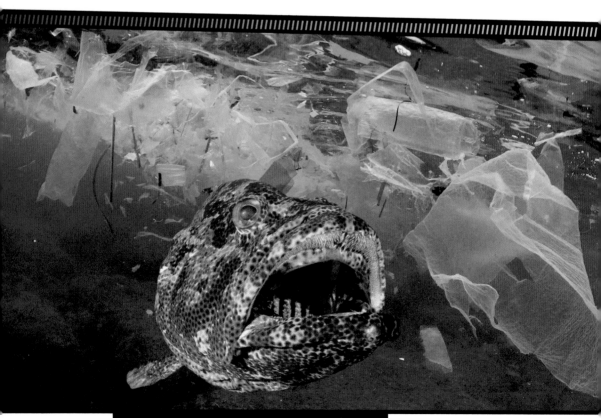

A grouper swims in polluted waters.

Global warming changes the water temperature. Warmer water makes the coral lose its color. This is called coral bleaching. Warmer seas put all marine life at risk. This includes groupers and moray eels.

A moray eel peaks out from damaged coral.

THE GROUPER

Also Known As: Varies by species

Species: Approximately 400 different species, including *Epinephelus itajara* (goliath) and *Cephalopholis fulva* (coney)

Size: Varies by species, 1–8 feet (0.3–2.4 m) long

Weight: Varies by species, 1–800 pounds (0.45–363 kg)

Skin: Varies by species, many colors and patterns

Features: Large, bulky body; large mouth; sharp, needlelike teeth; crushing tooth plates

As a Hunting Ally: Attracts a moray eel partner with rapid head shaking; hunts for prey in open water.

THE MORAY EEL

Also Known As: Varies by species

Species: Approximately 200 different species, including *Gymnothorax meleagris* (whitemouth) and *Gymnothorax funebris* (green)

Size: Varies by species, 3 inches (7.6 cm) to 10 feet (3 m) long

Weight: 1 ounce (28 grams) to 65 pounds (29 kg)

Skin: Varies by species, many colors and patterns

Features: Slender, snake-like body; extra set of teeth in throat; slimy mucus covers the body for protection

As a Hunting Ally: Squeezes into cracks and crevices to attack prey.

Glossary

aggressive (uh-GREH-siv)—ready to attack

camouflage (KA-muh-flahzh)—a pattern or color on an animal's skin that helps it blend in with the things around it

carnivore (KAHR-nuh-vohr)—an animal that eats only meat

collaborate (kuh-LAB-uh-rayt)—to work with others to complete a task

crustacean (kruss-TAY-shuhn)—a sea animal with an outer skeleton, such as a crab, lobster, or shrimp

food chain (FOOD CHAYN)—series of organisms in which each one in the series eats the one preceding it

mercury (MUR-kyuh-ree)—a poisonous metal that is liquid at ordinary temperatures

mucus (MYOO-khuss)—a slippery sticky substance produced especially by mucous membranes that it moistens and protects

mutualism (MYOO-choo-uhl-iz-um)—the kind of symbiosis that is good for both living things

nocturnal (nok-TUR-nuhl)—active at night

parasite (PAIR-uh-site)—an animal or plant that lives on or inside another animal or plant and causes harm

polyp (PAHL-ihp)— an animal or plant that lives on or inside another animal or plant and causes harm

symbiosis (sim-bye-OH-siss)—the close relationship between two or more different living things

Read More

Murphy, Macken. *Animal Sidekicks: Amazing Stories of Symbiosis in Animals and Plants*. New York: Neon Squid, 2022.

Rake, Jody S. *Kings of the Oceans*. North Mankato, MN: Capstone Press, 2018.

Ward, Jennifer. *Just You and Me: Remarkable Relationships in the Wild*. New York: Simon & Schuster, 2021.

Internet Sites

AZ Animals: Grouper
a-z-animals.com/animals/grouper/

National Aquarium: Green Moray Eel
aqua.org/explore/animals/green-moray-eel

National Geographic Kids: Ocean Facts!
natgeokids.com/uk/discover/geography/general-geography/ocean-facts/

Index

About the Author

A public and school librarian, Gloria Koster belongs to the Children's Book Committee of Bank Street College of Education. She enjoys both city and country life, dividing her time between Manhattan and the small town of Pound Ridge, New York. Gloria has three adult children and a bunch of energetic grandkids.